FRONT COVER PICTURE

Campanulas mingle with foxgloves to create a soft informal setting
Private Garden, Headley, Surrey
PHOTOGRAPH: PHOTOS HORTICULTURAL

BACK COVER PICTURE

Just enough room to sit and relax on this very small lawn, edged with rhododendrons
Private Garden, Norfolk
PHOTOGRAPH: ANNE GREEN-ARMYTAGE

ENDPAPERS

Seventeenth-century engraving for garden design
REPRODUCED BY COURTESY OF THE ROYAL HORTICULTURAL SOCIETY

OPPOSITE

A beautiful range of hues blended by designer Piet Oudolf
Pensthorpe Millenium Garden, Fakenham, Norfolk
PHOTOGRAPH: NEIL HOLMES

Published in England by

FOUR SEASONS
PUBLISHING

FOUR SEASONS PUBLISHING LIMITED
16 ORCHARD RISE, KINGSTON-UPON-THAMES, SURREY KT2 7EY

Designed and typeset by Judith Pedersen
Printed and bound in Singapore

© 2003 Four Seasons Publishing Ltd

ISBN 1 85645 166 6

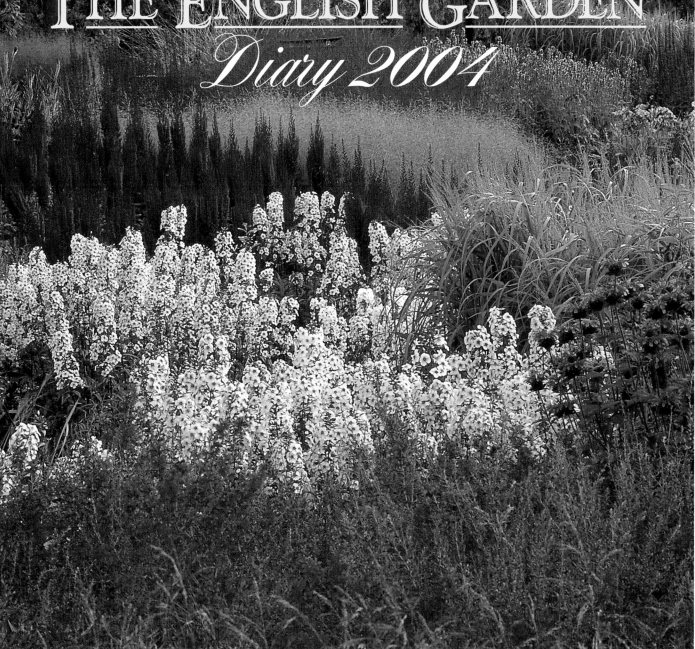

THE ENGLISH GARDEN
Diary 2004

2004

January

MONDAY	5	12	19	26
TUESDAY	6	13	20	27
WEDNESDAY	7	14	21	28
THURSDAY	1	8	15	22	29
FRIDAY	2	9	16	23	30
SATURDAY	3	10	17	24	31
SUNDAY	4	11	18	25

February

MONDAY	2	9	16	23
TUESDAY	3	10	17	24
WEDNESDAY	4	11	18	25
THURSDAY	5	12	19	26
FRIDAY	6	13	20	27
SATURDAY	7	14	21	28
SUNDAY	1	8	15	22	29

March

MONDAY	1	8	15	22	29
TUESDAY	2	9	16	23	30
WEDNESDAY	3	10	17	24	31
THURSDAY	4	11	18	25
FRIDAY	5	12	19	26
SATURDAY	6	13	20	27
SUNDAY	7	14	21	28

April

MONDAY	5	12	19	26
TUESDAY	6	13	20	27
WEDNESDAY	7	14	21	28
THURSDAY	1	8	15	22	29
FRIDAY	2	9	16	23	30
SATURDAY	3	10	17	24
SUNDAY	4	11	18	25

May

MONDAY	3	10	17	24	31
TUESDAY	4	11	18	25
WEDNESDAY	5	12	19	26
THURSDAY	6	13	20	27
FRIDAY	7	14	21	28
SATURDAY	1	8	15	22	29
SUNDAY	2	9	16	23	30

June

MONDAY	7	14	21	28
TUESDAY	1	8	15	22	29
WEDNESDAY	2	9	16	23	30
THURSDAY	3	10	17	24
FRIDAY	4	11	18	25
SATURDAY	5	12	19	26
SUNDAY	6	13	20	27

July

MONDAY	5	12	19	26
TUESDAY	6	13	20	27
WEDNESDAY	7	14	21	28
THURSDAY	1	8	15	22	29
FRIDAY	2	9	16	23	30
SATURDAY	3	10	17	24	31
SUNDAY	4	11	18	25

August

MONDAY	2	9	16	23	30
TUESDAY	3	10	17	24	31
WEDNESDAY	4	11	18	25
THURSDAY	5	12	19	26
FRIDAY	6	13	20	27
SATURDAY	7	14	21	28
SUNDAY	1	8	15	22	29

September

MONDAY	6	13	20	27
TUESDAY	7	14	21	28
WEDNESDAY	1	8	15	22	29
THURSDAY	2	9	16	23	30
FRIDAY	3	10	17	24
SATURDAY	4	11	18	25
SUNDAY	5	12	19	26

October

MONDAY	4	11	18	25
TUESDAY	5	12	19	26
WEDNESDAY	6	13	20	27
THURSDAY	7	14	21	28
FRIDAY	1	8	15	22	29
SATURDAY	2	9	16	23	30
SUNDAY	3	10	17	24	31

November

MONDAY	1	8	15	22	29
TUESDAY	2	9	16	23	30
WEDNESDAY	3	10	17	24
THURSDAY	4	11	18	25
FRIDAY	5	12	19	26
SATURDAY	6	13	20	27
SUNDAY	7	14	21	28

December

MONDAY	6	13	20	27
TUESDAY	7	14	21	28
WEDNESDAY	1	8	15	22	29
THURSDAY	2	9	16	23	30
FRIDAY	3	10	17	24	31
SATURDAY	4	11	18	25
SUNDAY	5	12	19	26

2005

January

MONDAY		3	10	17	24 31
TUESDAY		4	11	18	25
WEDNESDAY		5	12	19	26
THURSDAY		6	13	20	27
FRIDAY		7	14	21	28
SATURDAY	1	8	15	22	29
SUNDAY	2	9	16	23	30

February

MONDAY		7	14	21	28
TUESDAY	1	8	15	22	
WEDNESDAY	2	9	16	23	
THURSDAY	3	10	17	24	
FRIDAY	4	11	18	25	
SATURDAY	5	12	19	26	
SUNDAY	6	13	20	27	

March

MONDAY		7	14	21	28
TUESDAY	1	8	15	22	29
WEDNESDAY	2	9	16	23	30
THURSDAY	3	10	17	24	31
FRIDAY	4	11	18	25	
SATURDAY	5	12	19	26	
SUNDAY	6	13	20	27	

April

MONDAY		4	11	18	25
TUESDAY		5	12	19	26
WEDNESDAY		6	13	20	27
THURSDAY		7	14	21	28
FRIDAY	1	8	15	22	29
SATURDAY	2	9	16	23	30
SUNDAY	3	10	17	24	

May

MONDAY		2	9	16	23 30
TUESDAY		3	10	17	24 31
WEDNESDAY		4	11	18	25
THURSDAY		5	12	19	26
FRIDAY		6	13	20	27
SATURDAY		7	14	21	28
SUNDAY	1	8	15	22	29

June

MONDAY		6	13	20	27
TUESDAY		7	14	21	28
WEDNESDAY	1	8	15	22	29
THURSDAY	2	9	16	23	30
FRIDAY	3	10	17	24	
SATURDAY	4	11	18	25	
SUNDAY	5	12	19	26	

July

MONDAY		4	11	18	25
TUESDAY		5	12	19	26
WEDNESDAY		6	13	20	27
THURSDAY		7	14	21	28
FRIDAY	1	8	15	22	29
SATURDAY	2	9	16	23	30
SUNDAY	3	10	17	24	31

August

MONDAY	1	8	15	22	29
TUESDAY	2	9	16	23	30
WEDNESDAY	3	10	17	24	31
THURSDAY	4	11	18	25	
FRIDAY	5	12	19	26	
SATURDAY	6	13	20	27	
SUNDAY	7	14	21	28	

September

MONDAY		5	12	19	26
TUESDAY		6	13	20	27
WEDNESDAY		7	14	21	28
THURSDAY	1	8	15	22	29
FRIDAY	2	9	16	23	30
SATURDAY	3	10	17	24	
SUNDAY	4	11	18	25	

October

MONDAY		3	10	17	24 31
TUESDAY		4	11	18	25
WEDNESDAY		5	12	19	26
THURSDAY		6	13	20	27
FRIDAY		7	14	21	28
SATURDAY	1	8	15	22	29
SUNDAY	2	9	16	23	30

November

MONDAY		7	14	21	28
TUESDAY	1	8	15	22	29
WEDNESDAY	2	9	16	23	30
THURSDAY	3	10	17	24	
FRIDAY	4	11	18	25	
SATURDAY	5	12	19	26	
SUNDAY	6	13	20	27	

December

MONDAY		5	12	19	26
TUESDAY		6	13	20	27
WEDNESDAY		7	14	21	28
THURSDAY	1	8	15	22	29
FRIDAY	2	9	16	23	30
SATURDAY	3	10	17	24	31
SUNDAY	4	11	18	25	

December – January

29 MONDAY

30 TUESDAY

31 WEDNESDAY

1 THURSDAY   NEW YEAR'S DAY Bank Holiday, UK

Bank Holiday, Scotland   FRIDAY **2**

SATURDAY **3**

SUNDAY **4**

Bulbous heads of Allium hollandicum 'Purple Sensation' with a French variety of lavender
Royal Horticultural Society's Garden, Wisley, nr Ripley, Surrey

January

5 MONDAY

6 TUESDAY   EPIPHANY

7 WEDNESDAY

8 THURSDAY

FRIDAY **9**

SATURDAY **10**

SUNDAY **11**

A view across the frosted celtic knot garden, with its lollipop topiary
The Abbey House, Market Cross, Malmesbury, Wiltshire

January

12 <u>MONDAY</u>

13 <u>TUESDAY</u>

14 <u>WEDNESDAY</u>

15 <u>THURSDAY</u>

<u>FRIDAY</u> **16**

<u>SATURDAY</u> **17**

<u>SUNDAY</u> **18**

Just enough room to sit and relax on this very small lawn, edged with rhododendrons
Private Garden, Norfolk

January

19 MONDAY

20 TUESDAY

21 WEDNESDAY

22 THURSDAY

FRIDAY **23**

SATURDAY **24**

BURNS' NIGHT   SUNDAY **25**

January – February

26 <u>MONDAY</u>

27 <u>TUESDAY</u>

28 <u>WEDNESDAY</u>

29 <u>THURSDAY</u>

<u>FRIDAY</u> **30**

<u>SATURDAY</u> **31**

<u>SUNDAY</u> **1**

One of the many garden ornaments in this six-acre garden of outstanding beauty
Jenkyn Place, Bentley, nr Farnham, Hampshire

February

2 MONDAY

3 TUESDAY

4 WEDNESDAY

5 THURSDAY

Accession of HM Queen Elizabeth II

FRIDAY **6**

SATURDAY **7**

SUNDAY **8**

Winter-flowering Helleborus orientalis *and* Galanthus nivalus *in the shady garden*
Westacre Garden, nr Swaffham, Norfolk

February

9 <u>MONDAY</u>

10 <u>TUESDAY</u>

11 <u>WEDNESDAY</u>

12 <u>THURSDAY</u>

<u>FRIDAY</u> **13**

ST VALENTINE'S DAY   <u>SATURDAY</u> **14**

<u>SUNDAY</u> **15**

A glasshouse which supplies the arrangements of cut flowers for which the house is famous
Parham House, Pulborough, West Sussex

John Glover

February

16 <u>MONDAY</u>

17 <u>TUESDAY</u>

18 <u>WEDNESDAY</u>

19 <u>THURSDAY</u>

<u>FRIDAY</u> **20**

<u>SATURDAY</u> **21**

<u>SUNDAY</u> **22**

A recently laid out knot garden of box and germander flanked by yew
Antony House, Torpoint, Cornwall

February

23 MONDAY

24 TUESDAY   SHROVE TUESDAY

25 WEDNESDAY   ASH WEDNESDAY

26 THURSDAY

FRIDAY **27**

SATURDAY **28**

SUNDAY **29**

White and pink feathery spires and purple salvia stir in the breeze
Private Garden, nr Oakham, Leicestershire

March

1 MONDAY   ST DAVID'S DAY   FRIDAY 5

2 TUESDAY   SATURDAY 6

3 WEDNESDAY   SUNDAY 7

4 THURSDAY

Field poppies catch the sun and early morning dew
Private Garden, Norfolk

Anne Green-Armytage

March

8 <u>MONDAY</u>   COMMONWEALTH DAY

<u>FRIDAY</u> **12**

9 <u>TUESDAY</u>

<u>SATURDAY</u> **13**

10 <u>WEDNESDAY</u>

<u>SUNDAY</u> **14**

11 <u>THURSDAY</u>

Borders of tulips and forget-me-nots with the greenhouse and kitchen garden behind
Pashley Manor Garden, nr Ticehurst, East Sussex

March

15 MONDAY

16 TUESDAY

17 WEDNESDAY   ST PATRICK'S DAY Bank Holiday, N. Ireland

18 THURSDAY

FRIDAY **19**

06.41 hrs GMT Vernal Equinox (Spring begins)   SATURDAY **20**

MOTHERING SUNDAY   SUNDAY **21**

Herbaceous borders full of good plantings, originally Gertrude Jekyll's own garden
Munstead Wood, Busbridge, Godalming, Surrey

John Glover

March

22 MONDAY

23 TUESDAY

24 WEDNESDAY

25 THURSDAY

FRIDAY **26**

SATURDAY **27**

British Summer Time begins (clocks forward 1 hr)   SUNDAY **28**

These hidden gardens are a surprise to be found 300 metres up in the Pennines
Dunge Valley Gardens, High Peak, Cheshire

March – April

29 MONDAY

30 TUESDAY

31 WEDNESDAY

1 THURSDAY   APRIL FOOL'S DAY

FRIDAY **2**

SATURDAY **3**

PALM SUNDAY   SUNDAY **4**

A view across the lawn and topiary from an open window
The Old Manor, Hemingford Grey, Huntingdon, Cambridgeshire

Marianne Majerus

April

5 <u>MONDAY</u>

GOOD FRIDAY Bank Holiday, UK   <u>FRIDAY</u> **9**

6 <u>TUESDAY</u>

<u>SATURDAY</u> **10**

7 <u>WEDNESDAY</u>

EASTER SUNDAY   <u>SUNDAY</u> **11**

8 <u>THURSDAY</u>   MAUNDY THURSDAY

The rose garden, designed by Christina Williams, the owner's daughter
Coughton Court, Alcester, Warwickshire

Andrew Lawson

April

12 MONDAY
EASTER MONDAY Bank Holiday, UK not Scotland

13 TUESDAY

14 WEDNESDAY

15 THURSDAY

FRIDAY 16

SATURDAY 17

SUNDAY 18

A double border of yellow and white hostas shaded by an avenue of beeches
Hadspen Gardens, Castle Cary, Somerset

Mark Bolton

April

19 MONDAY

20 TUESDAY

21 WEDNESDAY   Birthday of HM Queen Elizabeth II

22 THURSDAY

ST GEORGE'S DAY   FRIDAY **23**

SATURDAY **24**

SUNDAY **25**

Ancient sculptured box hedges with agapanthus
Belmore House, Upham, Hampshire

April – May

26 MONDAY

27 TUESDAY

28 WEDNESDAY

29 THURSDAY

FRIDAY **30**

SATURDAY **1**

SUNDAY **2**

May

3 <u>MONDAY</u> May Day Bank Holiday, UK

4 <u>TUESDAY</u>

5 <u>WEDNESDAY</u>

6 <u>THURSDAY</u>

<u>FRIDAY</u> **7**

<u>SATURDAY</u> **8**

<u>SUNDAY</u> **9**

A *charming courtyard garden with* Narcissus 'Pipit' *and* Tulipa 'Marilyn'
The Old Vicarage, Carbrooke, Norfolk

May

10 <u>MONDAY</u>

<u>FRIDAY</u> 14

11 <u>TUESDAY</u>

<u>SATURDAY</u> 15

12 <u>WEDNESDAY</u>

<u>SUNDAY</u> 16

13 <u>THURSDAY</u>

A tree painted vivid blue provides a stunning focal point
Private Garden, Oxfordshire

May

17 <u>MONDAY</u>

<u>FRIDAY</u> **21**

18 <u>TUESDAY</u>

<u>SATURDAY</u> **22**

19 <u>WEDNESDAY</u>

<u>SUNDAY</u> **23**

20 <u>THURSDAY</u>   ASCENSION DAY

The lily pond, topiary seat and summer house in an organic garden
Abbey Cottage, Itchen Abbas, Hampshire

May

24 <u>MONDAY</u>

<u>FRIDAY</u> **28**

25 <u>TUESDAY</u>

<u>SATURDAY</u> **29**

26 <u>WEDNESDAY</u>

WHIT SUNDAY   <u>SUNDAY</u> **30**

27 <u>THURSDAY</u>

Iris, allium and verbascum flanked by hornbeams
Chelsea Flower Show, London

May – June

31 MONDAY   Spring Bank Holiday, UK

FRIDAY **4**

1 TUESDAY

SATURDAY **5**

2 WEDNESDAY   CORONATION DAY

TRINITY SUNDAY   SUNDAY **6**

3 THURSDAY

Bluebells and deciduous azaleas make a truly magnificent palette of colour
Leonardslee, Lower Beeding, Horsham, West Sussex

June

7 <u>MONDAY</u>

8 <u>TUESDAY</u>

9 <u>WEDNESDAY</u>

10 <u>THURSDAY</u>

<u>FRIDAY</u> **11**

<u>SATURDAY</u> **12**

<u>SUNDAY</u> **13**

Horizontal stripes of colourful bedding in front of the sixteenth-century house
Southover Grange Gardens, Lewes, East Sussex

David Sellman

June

14 MONDAY

15 TUESDAY

16 WEDNESDAY

17 THURSDAY

FRIDAY **18**

SATURDAY **19**

FATHER'S DAY   SUNDAY **20**

Water descends through several levels, surrounded by Rosa 'The Fairy'
Wollerton Old Hall, Wollerton, Market Drayton, Shropshire

June

21 <u>MONDAY</u>

00.48 hrs GMT Summer Solstice
(longest day of the year)

<u>FRIDAY</u> **25**

22 <u>TUESDAY</u>

<u>SATURDAY</u> **26**

23 <u>WEDNESDAY</u>

<u>SUNDAY</u> **27**

24 <u>THURSDAY</u>

This post office makes a traditional 'picture postcard' image
Sherborne Post Office, Sherborne, Gloucestershire

June – July

28 <u>MONDAY</u>

29 <u>TUESDAY</u>

30 <u>WEDNESDAY</u>

1 <u>THURSDAY</u>

<u>FRIDAY</u> **2**

<u>SATURDAY</u> **3**

<u>SUNDAY</u> **4**

A well-cared-for knot garden on a bank above the River Test
Houghton Lodge Gardens, Stockbridge, Hampshire

July

5 MONDAY

FRIDAY 9

6 TUESDAY

SATURDAY 10

7 WEDNESDAY

SUNDAY 11

8 THURSDAY

Tulip-filled containers grace this city garden
Malvern Terrace, London

July

12 <u>MONDAY</u>   Bank Holiday, N. Ireland

13 <u>TUESDAY</u>

14 <u>WEDNESDAY</u>

15 <u>THURSDAY</u>

<u>FRIDAY</u> **16**

<u>SATURDAY</u> **17**

<u>SUNDAY</u> **18**

Rows of cannas from America give a tropical feel to this garden
Desert World, Thetford Forest, Suffolk

July

19 MONDAY

20 TUESDAY

21 WEDNESDAY

22 THURSDAY

FRIDAY **23**

SATURDAY **24**

SUNDAY **25**

A view to admire across the ocean, from this cliff-top garden
Private Garden, Dawlish, Devon

Andrew Lawson

July – August

26 MONDAY

27 TUESDAY

28 WEDNESDAY

29 THURSDAY

FRIDAY **30**

SATURDAY **31**

SUNDAY **1**

Crimson tulips grow beside terracotta rhubarb forcing pots
Private Garden, Somerset

August

2 MONDAY   Summer Bank Holiday, Scotland   FRIDAY **6**

3 TUESDAY   SATURDAY **7**

4 WEDNESDAY   SUNDAY **8**

5 THURSDAY

A pathway leads through the apple pergola and lavender bushes to the lake
Brookwell, Birtley Green, Surrey

August

9 <u>MONDAY</u>

<u>FRIDAY</u> 13

10 <u>TUESDAY</u>

<u>SATURDAY</u> 14

11 <u>WEDNESDAY</u>

<u>SUNDAY</u> 15

12 <u>THURSDAY</u>

Campanulas mingle with foxgloves to create a soft informal setting
Private Garden, Headley, Surrey

August

16 MONDAY

17 TUESDAY

18 WEDNESDAY

19 THURSDAY

FRIDAY **20**

SATURDAY **21**

SUNDAY **22**

A railway runs alongside this small cottage garden, which contains many alpine plants
The Crossing House, Shepreth, Cambridgeshire

David Coleman

August

23 MONDAY

24 TUESDAY

25 WEDNESDAY

26 THURSDAY

FRIDAY **27**

SATURDAY **28**

SUNDAY **29**

Deep pink feathery spires of astilbe blend with the daisy-like flowers of echinacea
Private Garden, nr Bury St Edmunds, Suffolk

Neil Holmes

August – September

30 MONDAY   Late Summer Bank Holiday, UK not Scotland

31 TUESDAY

1 WEDNESDAY

2 THURSDAY

FRIDAY **3**

SATURDAY **4**

SUNDAY **5**

Mixed primulas flower next to the distinctive forms of Euphorbia 'Humpty Dumpty'
Windy Ridge, Bolton Percy, nr Tadcaster, Yorkshire

September

6 <u>MONDAY</u>

7 <u>TUESDAY</u>

8 <u>WEDNESDAY</u>

9 <u>THURSDAY</u>

<u>FRIDAY</u> **10**

<u>SATURDAY</u> **11**

<u>SUNDAY</u> **12**

Gentle wooden steps dissect this garden, designed by James Hitchmough and Amanda Stokes
Private Garden, Sheffield, South Yorkshire

September

13 <u>MONDAY</u>

14 <u>TUESDAY</u>

15 <u>WEDNESDAY</u>

16 <u>THURSDAY</u>

<u>FRIDAY</u> **17**

<u>SATURDAY</u> **18**

<u>SUNDAY</u> **19**

The exceptional views at dawn from this one-acre garden create an illusion of great space
Pettifers Garden, Lower Wardington, Oxfordshire

September

20 MONDAY

FRIDAY 24

21 TUESDAY

SATURDAY 25

22 WEDNESDAY   16.25 hrs GMT Autumn Equinox (Autumn begins)

SUNDAY 26

23 THURSDAY

Large brightly-coloured dahlias in a variety of forms nestle between the stone walls
Fleetlands Farm, Shalfleet, Isle of Wight

September – October

27 <u>MONDAY</u>

28 <u>TUESDAY</u>

29 <u>WEDNESDAY</u>

30 <u>THURSDAY</u>

<u>FRIDAY</u> **1**

<u>SATURDAY</u> **2**

<u>SUNDAY</u> **3**

Autumnal colours tinge the leaves of the azaleas and ferns
Arley Hall, Northwick, Cheshire

October

4 MONDAY

5 TUESDAY

6 WEDNESDAY

7 THURSDAY

FRIDAY **8**

SATURDAY **9**

SUNDAY **10**

Spiky-leafed succulents create a desert-like garden
Old Vicarage, East Rushton, nr Norwich, Norfolk

Neil Holmes

October

11 MONDAY

12 TUESDAY

13 WEDNESDAY

14 THURSDAY

FRIDAY **15**

SATURDAY **16**

SUNDAY **17**

Colin Roberts

October

18 <u>MONDAY</u>

FRIDAY 22

19 <u>TUESDAY</u>

<u>SATURDAY</u> 23

20 <u>WEDNESDAY</u>

<u>SUNDAY</u> 24

21 <u>THURSDAY</u>

Marianne Majerus

October

25 MONDAY

FRIDAY 29

26 TUESDAY

SATURDAY 30

27 WEDNESDAY

HALLOWEEN
British Summer Time ends (clocks back 1 hr)

SUNDAY 31

28 THURSDAY

Many beautiful cottage gardens can be visited in this Cotswold village
Private Garden, Blockley, nr Moreton-in-the-Marsh, Gloucestershire

John Glover

November

1 <u>MONDAY</u>

2 <u>TUESDAY</u>

3 <u>WEDNESDAY</u>

4 <u>THURSDAY</u>

GUY FAWKES NIGHT

<u>FRIDAY</u> **5**

<u>SATURDAY</u> **6**

<u>SUNDAY</u> **7**

Winter containers take on an almost sculptural appearance
Private Garden, Oxfordshire

Andrew Lawson

November

8 <u>MONDAY</u>

<u>FRIDAY</u> **12**

9 <u>TUESDAY</u>

<u>SATURDAY</u> **13**

10 <u>WEDNESDAY</u>

REMEMBRANCE SUNDAY   <u>SUNDAY</u> **14**

11 <u>THURSDAY</u>

Karen Frenkel

November

15 <u>MONDAY</u>

<u>FRIDAY</u> **19**

16 <u>TUESDAY</u>

<u>SATURDAY</u> **20**

17 <u>WEDNESDAY</u>

<u>SUNDAY</u> **21**

18 <u>THURSDAY</u>

The modern stainless-steel water feature contrasts with more traditional features in this garden
Tatton Park, Knutsford, Cheshire

Dave Bevan

November

22 <u>MONDAY</u>

23 <u>TUESDAY</u>

24 <u>WEDNESDAY</u>

25 <u>THURSDAY</u>

<u>FRIDAY</u> **26**

<u>SATURDAY</u> **27**

ADVENT SUNDAY   <u>SUNDAY</u> **28**

Spires of contrasting yellow and blue flowers in this cottage garden
Garden House Farm, Drinkstone, Suffolk

Jerry Harpur

November – December

29 MONDAY

30 TUESDAY   ST ANDREW'S DAY

1 WEDNESDAY

2 THURSDAY

FRIDAY **3**

SATURDAY **4**

SUNDAY **5**

The vast Italian parterre, covered with frost
Penshurst Place, Penshurst, Kent

December

6 <u>MONDAY</u>

7 <u>TUESDAY</u>

8 <u>WEDNESDAY</u>

9 <u>THURSDAY</u>

<u>FRIDAY</u> **10**

<u>SATURDAY</u> **11**

<u>SUNDAY</u> **12**

David Sellman

December

13 <u>MONDAY</u>

14 <u>TUESDAY</u>

15 <u>WEDNESDAY</u>

16 <u>THURSDAY</u>

<u>FRIDAY</u> **17**

<u>SATURDAY</u> **18**

<u>SUNDAY</u> **19**

December

20 MONDAY

FRIDAY **24**

21 TUESDAY

12.41 hrs GMT Winter Solstice
(shortest day of the year)

CHRISTMAS DAY

SATURDAY **25**

22 WEDNESDAY

BOXING DAY

SUNDAY **26**

23 THURSDAY

Clusters of red berries of Cotoneaster 'Cornubia', topped with an icing of snow
Holkham Gardens, nr Wells, Norfolk

Neil Holmes

December – January

27 <u>MONDAY</u>   Bank Holiday, UK

28 <u>TUESDAY</u>   Bank Holiday, UK

29 <u>WEDNESDAY</u>

30 <u>THURSDAY</u>

<u>FRIDAY</u> **31**

NEW YEAR'S DAY   <u>SATURDAY</u> **1**

<u>SUNDAY</u> **2**

The chimneys of the imposing stone house are reflected in the pool
Borde Hill Garden, Haywards Heath, West Sussex

David Sellman

Addresses

NAME

ADDRESS

TELEPHONE

MOBILE

NAME

ADDRESS

TELEPHONE

MOBILE

NAME

ADDRESS

TELEPHONE

MOBILE

NAME

ADDRESS

TELEPHONE

MOBILE

NAME

ADDRESS

TELEPHONE

MOBILE

NAME

ADDRESS

TELEPHONE

MOBILE

NAME

ADDRESS

TELEPHONE

MOBILE

NAME

ADDRESS

TELEPHONE

MOBILE

Addresses

NAME

ADDRESS

TELEPHONE

MOBILE

NAME

ADDRESS

TELEPHONE

MOBILE

NAME

ADDRESS

TELEPHONE

MOBILE

NAME

ADDRESS

TELEPHONE

MOBILE

NAME

ADDRESS

TELEPHONE

MOBILE

NAME

ADDRESS

TELEPHONE

MOBILE

NAME

ADDRESS

TELEPHONE

MOBILE

NAME

ADDRESS

TELEPHONE

MOBILE

Notes

Notes